Word Processor Training Guides

WordPerfect Release 5.0

GW00600647

Anne Clark and Kath Butler

HOUNSLOW BOROUGH COLLEGE
BUSINESS STUDIES DEPT.
LONDON ROAD, ISLEWORTH, MIDDX, TW7 4HS

Pitman

B49

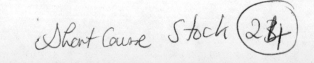
Short Course Stock 28

PITMAN PUBLISHING
128 Long Acre, London WC2E 9AN

A Division of Longman Group UK Limited

© Anne Clark and Kath Butler 1990

First published in Great Britain 1990
Reprinted 1990

British Library Cataloguing in Publication Data

Clark, (Anne),
  Wordperfect
  1. Word processing. Software packages.
  I. Title II. Butler, (Kath)
  III. Series
  652'.5'028553

ISBN 0 273 03261 5

All rights reserved; no part of this publication may be reproduced,
stored in a retrieval system, or transmitted in any form or by any
means, electronic, mechanical, photocopying, recording, or otherwise
without either the prior written permission of the Publishers or a
licence permitting restricted copying in the United Kingdom issued by
the Copyright Licensing Agency Ltd, 33-34 Alfred Place, London,
WC1E 7DP. This book may not be lent, resold, hired out or
otherwise disposed of by way of trade in any form of binding or
cover other than that in which it is published, without the prior
consent of the Publishers.

Typeset in 10/12 Futura by 𝆑 Tek Art Limited, Croydon, Surrey
Printed and bound in Singapore

Acknowledgement
WordPerfect is a registered trademark of WordPerfect Corporation,
1555 Technology Way, Orem, Utah 84057, USA.

Contents

Introduction 1
Getting started 2

Introduction

The tasks in this training guide are intended to introduce the new WordPerfect user to the facilities of the system in a practical manner.

Working the tasks   Material to be typed is enclosed in a solid box to distinguish it from other information or instructions. The tasks start with the assumption that the microcomputer is already switched on and that a printer is attached if any immediate printout is required.

Getting started

Before using WordPerfect, refer to the manufacturer's manual for details on setting up the computer, monitor and printer and copying the master disks. You will need a formatted blank disk for your work disk.

Hard disk system   Switch on the computer. Follow any screen prompts until C> appears onscreen. Change to the WordPerfect directory (you will probably type `cd\wp50` and press `RETURN`). Type `wp` and press `RETURN` to load the program. (*Note*   RETURN is shown as ENTER or `↵` on some keyboards.)

Two floppy disk system   Switch on the computer and place the DOS disk in drive A. Follow any screen prompts until A> appears onscreen. Remove the DOS disk and replace it with the WordPerfect System 1 disk. Type `wp` and press `RETURN` to load the program. You may now need to replace the WordPerfect System 1 disk with the WordPerfect System 2 disk.

The screen shows the area where you will type.

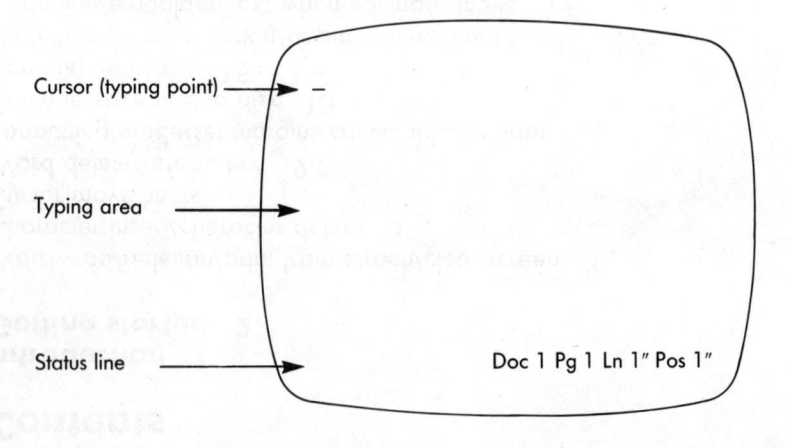

Cursor (typing point) ———

Typing area ———

Status line ———

Doc 1 Pg 1 Ln 1" Pos 1"

The **cursor** (which is roughly the equivalent of the printing point on a typewriter) moves across the screen as text is typed. It can be moved around the screen by using the arrow keys that point up, down, right and left.

The **status line** tells you which document you are working on (1 of 2), the page and line number where the cursor is and the cursor position across the page (there is a pre-set 1 inch left margin).

Insert work disk
Insert your formatted work disk into drive A (hard disk system) or drive B (two floppy disk system).

Keyboard template
A template is provided with your manual describing which function keys are used to perform which function. Depending on the layout of your keyboard, you will need to place the template around the Function keys (F keys). These functions are colour coded and each key can be pressed alone, in conjunction with the Ctrl (control), Shift (⇧) or Alt keys. Remember to hold down the CTRL, ALT or SHIFT key, then press the appropriate F key, and then release both keys.

Key	With CTRL	With SHIFT	With ALT	Alone
F1	Shell	Setup	Thesaurus	Cancel
F2	Spell	Search	Replace	Search
F3	Screen	Switch	Reveal Codes*	Help
F4	Move	Indent	Block*	Indent
F5	Text In/Out	Date/Outline	Mark Text	List Files
F6	Tab Align	Centre	Flush Right	Bold
F7	Footnote	Print	Math/Columns	Exit
F8	Font	Format	Style	Underline
F9	Merge/Sort	Merge Codes	Graphics	Merge R
F10	Macro Del	Retrieve	Macro	Save
F11				Reveal Codes*
F12				Block*

*If you have an enhanced keyboard with F11 and F12 keys, it is easier to use these instead of Alt F3 and Alt F4.

Place the template round your keys ready for use when instructed.

Task 1

Objective   To input text, observe the wordwrap feature, make running corrections and print.

Wordwrap   When typing in text, do not press RETURN at the ends of lines as on a typewriter – WordPerfect will make its own line endings. Only press RETURN when a new paragraph is required.

Deletion   If you type a wrong letter and notice it immediately, use the backspace delete key (marked ← and located above the RETURN key) to remove the character to the left, and then retype. Other ways of correction will be described in later tasks.

Print from screen
1 Hold down SHIFT and press F7.
2 Press 2 (to print the page).

Clear screen
1 Press F7 (to exit).
2 Press N (not to save).
3 Press N (not to exit WP).

Memory jogger   The cursor is the typing point.

Text creation
1 Type Your Own Name (to identify printout).
2 Press RETURN three times.
3 Type in the text of Task 1, remembering to press RETURN twice between paragraphs to leave a blank line space.

Amendments   No special amendments, but read through your work – on this occasion leave any errors which you did not correct when typing in the text. Print your work from screen. Then clear screen (see above) ready for Task 2.

Task 1

Getting used to the keyboard of a word processor is fairly easy. The letters of the alphabet are set out as on a typewriter but you will probably find that other keys are different from those that you are used to seeing on a typewriter.

You may find that there are keys with arrows on them for moving the cursor around the screen. The numbers may be on a separate number pad - probably on the right. There may be other keys which have names on them which will allow you to do specific functions.

Some machines have a 'CAPS LOCK' key as well as a SHIFT key. The SHIFT key when depressed allows you to get capital letters and the special signs which are on the top row of the figure or punctuation keys. The CAPS LOCK allows you to type in capital letters, but, if you press a key with two symbols on it, you will still get the lower one.

All machines differ in the layout and number of the special keys, so it is a useful activity to spend some time familiarising yourself with your particular keyboard.

Task 2

Objective   To insert and delete characters in text.

Character insert	Position the cursor at the point where you want the additional character(s) to appear and type them in. For additional space tap the SPACE BAR.
Character delete	Position the cursor on the unwanted character or space and then press $\boxed{\text{DEL} \rightarrow}$ (on far right of bottom line of keyboard).

Memory joggers

1 **Wordwrap:** only press the $\boxed{\text{RETURN}}$ key when you want to start a new paragraph – WordPerfect will make the line endings within each paragraph.
2 **Cursor:** use the cursor movement (arrow) keys to move the cursor over your text when checking or editing – if you use the space bar to move the cursor across the screen, you will insert spaces; if you use the $\boxed{\text{RETURN}}$ key to move down, you will insert line spaces.

Text creation

1 Type $\boxed{\text{Your Own Name}}$ (to identify printout).
2 Press $\boxed{\text{RETURN}}$ three times.
3 Type in the text of Task 2, remembering to press $\boxed{\text{RETURN}}$ twice between paragraphs.

Amendments

Now make some changes to the text you have just typed:

1 First paragraph, first sentence: change 'a printed document' into 'printed documents' (delete 'a' and the space after it and type in 's' at the end of 'document').
2 Second paragraph, second sentence: change 'complete retypes' to 'a complete retype' (insert 'a' plus a space before the word 'complete'; delete the 's' at the end of 'retypes').
3 Second paragraph, last three words: change 'modern office workers' to 'the modern office worker'.
4 Third paragraph: change 'legal offices' to 'a legal office'.

Check your work, correcting any remaining errors. Print your work from screen and then clear the screen (see page 59).

Task 2

Word processing simply means transferring thoughts into a printed
document as speedily and efficiently as possible. Not that many years
ago this meant that a secretary copy typed handwritten material, took
shorthand dictation or used an audio tape and transcribed that,
usually using a manual typewriter.

The working life of the secretary improved somewhat with the advent of
electric typewriters but this still meant that repetitive work had to
be retyped whenever required. It also still meant complete retypes if
errors were made towards the bottom of a full page of typescript -
with the possibility of making those same mistakes again. The
introduction of word processing systems has done much to remove these
unsatisfactory elements and increase job satisfaction for modern
office workers.

Owing to its ability to store material, a word processing system is
particularly useful for such repetitive work as is found in legal
offices where standard paragraphs and clauses can be stored for
constant recall.

Another important advantage is that, once checked, material recalled
from store need not be checked again. Great time savings can thus be
made by only having to make sure that the additions or other
amendments have been made to a document.

Task 3

Objective   To operate fast cursor movements.

Cursor movements	1 Hold $\boxed{\text{CTRL}}$ and press $\boxed{\rightarrow}$ or $\boxed{\leftarrow}$ to move one word right or left.
	2 Press $\boxed{\text{END}}$ to move to end of line.
	3 Press $\boxed{\text{Pg Up}}$ to move to top of page.
	4 Press $\boxed{\text{Pg Dn}}$ to move to bottom of page.
	5 Press $\boxed{\text{HOME}}$ and $\boxed{\uparrow}$ arrow to move to top of screen.
	6 Press $\boxed{\text{HOME}}$ and $\boxed{\downarrow}$ arrow to move to bottom of screen.
	7 Press $\boxed{\text{HOME}}$ $\boxed{\text{HOME}}$ and $\boxed{\uparrow}$ arrow to move to beginning of file.
	8 Press $\boxed{\text{HOME}}$ $\boxed{\text{HOME}}$ and $\boxed{\downarrow}$ arrow to move to end of file.

Memory joggers

1 Pressing the $\boxed{\text{SPACE BAR}}$ inserts spaces.
2 Pressing the $\boxed{\text{RETURN}}$ key inserts line spaces.
3 Arrow keys move the cursor around the screen in the direction of the arrows.

Text creation

1 Type $\boxed{\text{Your Own Name}}$ (to identify printout).
2 Press $\boxed{\text{RETURN}}$ three times.
3 Type in the text of Task 2, remembering to press $\boxed{\text{RETURN}}$ twice between paragraphs.

Amendments

1 Before checking your work, practise using all the fast cursor movements shown above.
2 Print one copy from screen and clear the screen (see page 59).

Task 3

The equipment found in the postal section or mailroom of an
organisation varies a great deal according to the size of the firm and
the volume of post it handles each day.

In the smallest office postal activities may be handled by one person
as a part of their total duties, and the 'equipment' may comprise
merely a weighing scale, an up to date copy of the Post Office Guide,
and a batch of postage stamps. The medium sized firm might have a
franking machine, more staff help and perhaps a package-tying machine
for putting string or tape round parcels.

The range of equipment available to the larger firms who need it,
however, goes much further than this. There are inserting and mailing
machines, which mechanise the whole procedure of collating papers,
opening envelope flaps and then sealing, franking with the postage
impressions and stacking envelopes.

Even the ubiquitous weighing scales are now available in an updated,
computerised form. The item to be posted is placed on the scale
platform, a panel on the front is touched for the relevant destination
area, plus any special requirements such as Swiftair, and the readout
displays the amount needed for postage.

Obviously this type of electronic scale has to be programmed with
current postage rates and when there is a change the manufacturer has
to reprogram it accordingly.

Task 4

Objective   To use the word delete function and reform text.

Word delete   1 Position the cursor at the beginning of the unwanted word.
2 Hold down $\boxed{\text{CTRL}}$ and press the $\boxed{\text{BACKSPACE DELETE}}$ ($\boxed{\leftarrow}$) key (above the RETURN key).
3 The unwanted word will be removed and the text will close up so as not to leave a gap.

Reform text   After editing, move the cursor down through the text to reform it to the margin settings.

Memory joggers   1 Use the arrow keys to move the cursor over the text.
2 Use the $\boxed{\text{HOME}}$ and $\boxed{\uparrow}$ or $\boxed{\downarrow}$ keys to move to the top/bottom of the screen.

Text creation   1 Type $\boxed{\text{Your Own Name}}$ (to identify printout).
2 Press $\boxed{\text{RETURN}}$ three times.
3 Type in the text of Task 4, remembering to press $\boxed{\text{RETURN}}$ twice between paragraphs.

Amendments   Make the following changes:

1 First paragraph, first line: delete the word 'world's' in the 'world's smallest word processor'.
2 Second paragraph, first sentence: delete 'keys' in 'has only six keys'.
3 Second paragraph, second sentence: delete 'alphabetic' in 'alphabetic letters on them'.
4 Second paragraph, second sentence: delete 'special' in 'certain special combinations'.
5 Third paragraph, last line: delete 'very' in 'very much easier'.

Check your work and make any necessary corrections. Then print one copy from screen and clear the screen (see page 59).

Task 4

A Microwriter is probably the world's smallest word processor available
at present. It can be held in one hand and weighs about a kilogram.

Whereas most word processing systems have rows of keys set out on a
keyboard, the Microwriter has only six keys which are set out roughly
in the shape of the hand - four being used by the fingers and two by
the thumb. These keys do not have alphabetic letters on them but can
be pressed in certain special combinations, causing characters to
appear in the 'thin window' display area at the top.

The memory in a Microwriter is not lost when the machine is switched
off so an executive can key in his or her own notes when away from the
office and, on return, connect the Microwriter to a printer or
electronic typewriter and obtain printed documents. It is also
possible to connect it to a television set and see several lines of
text on the screen, which can make the editing task very much easier.

Task 5

Objective   To specify own margins and tab stops.

Formatting mode   The Tab Ruler shows the current margin and tab settings.
Tabs are pre-set every 5 characters starting from position 16.

1 Display Tab Ruler: hold CTRL and press F3. Press 1 (for window), press ↑ arrow once and RETURN (to set the ruler).
2 Remove Tab Ruler: hold CTRL and press F3. Press 1 (for window), press ↓ arrow once and RETURN.

Set margins   Set margin: hold SHIFT and press F8. Press 1 (for line), press 7 (for margins), then type the number for the new left margin. Press RETURN. Type the number for the new right margin and press RETURN three times.

Cancel tabs   Cancel all tabs: hold SHIFT and press F8. Press 1 (line), press 8 (tab), place the cursor on 0″ on the scale, hold down CTRL and press END. Press F7 twice to exit.

Set tabs   Set tab: hold SHIFT and press F8. Press 1 (line), press 8 (tab), type the value of the tab to be set (eg 4.5) and press RETURN, press F7 twice.

Memory jogger   When a tab has been set, move to it by pressing the tab key ⇆ (on the left of the keyboard).

Text creation   1 Type Your Own Name (to identify printout).
2 Press RETURN three times.
3 Set the left margin at 1.5″, the right margin at 1.5″ and a tab stop at 4.5″.
4 Type in the text of Task 5, remembering to press the TAB key (⇆) to reach the figure column when typing in the material.

Amendments   There are no amendments but check your work, correcting any errors. Print one copy from screen and clear the screen (see page 59).

Task 5

CHAIRMAN'S REPORT

In presenting the Annual Report for 19--/- at the London Hilton Hotel, the Chairman said: 'There is a worldwide demand for goods of high quality and value and there is no reason why they should not be made in Britain. Our increased sales both at home and overseas demonstrates this clearly.'

GROUP RESULTS

	value (£ million)
Group total	2505.5
UK stores	2276.2
Direct export sales	27.6
Overseas stores	201.7
Group profit	135.2

In conclusion, the Chairman said: 'We believe that the problems facing our community today cannot be solved by Government alone. Business has a responsibility which goes well beyond paying taxes, and last year our contribution to community work cost more than £3 million. We believe this to be a valuable investment.'

Task 6

Objective	To centre headings; save files to disk.

Centring	1 Hold down the SHIFT key and press F6.
	2 Type the word(s) to be centred. Press RETURN. The word(s) will be centred when the cursor moves down the text.
	To remove centring: place the cursor on the first space after the centred text. Press DEL. In answer to the prompt, press Y.
Save files to disk	Press F7. Press RETURN (to save). Name the file by typing the drive letter, then a colon, followed by a name (maximum 8 characters). It is useful to use your initials, eg Janet Freeman would be b:JF6 (twin floppy disk system) or a:JF6 (hard disk system).

Memory jogger	Do not press RETURN at the end of a line unless it is the end of a paragraph.
Text creation	1 Type Your Own Name (to identify printout).
	2 Press RETURN three times.
	3 Type in the text of Task 6, remembering to press RETURN twice between paragraphs.
Amendments	1 Remove centring from headings.
	2 If extra practice is required, centre headings again by putting the cursor on the first character and pressing SHIFT and F6.
	Check your work and make any necessary corrections. Save your work under filename YourInitials6 and print one copy from disk (see page 59).

Task 6

RUNNING COSTS

It should not be forgotten that word processing systems have other than
initial costs. Usually a maintenance contract is signed to keep the
equipment in good order and this amounts to about 10% of the
installation cost. This has to be paid each year.

CONSUMABLES

There are smaller items connected with word processing which must also
be considered. These can be called consumables and include such things
as paper, printer ribbons, the print element (such as a daisy wheel,
which will need replacing) and disks for storage.

PRINTER RIBBONS

The life of a single-strike ribbon, for example, used for high quality
printing, is its length times the character pitch. Thus a 300 ft
ribbon, used for 10-pitch printing, will last for 36 000 characters -
approximately nine A4 pages.

RIBBON COSTS

If the ribbon costs £5, this means each page costs about 55p for the
ribbon alone. It is not surprising to find multi-strike ribbons often
being used.

Task 7

Objective   To centre a document vertically.

<table>
<tr><td>Centring
vertically</td><td>After keying in the whole text return to the beginning of the file by pressing HOME HOME and ↑. Hold down SHIFT key and press F8. Answer the questions by pressing 2 (page), 1 (centre page: top to bottom) and then press RETURN twice (to return to document).

Note   The text on the screen does not change but it will be centred when it is printed out.</td></tr>
</table>

Memory jogger   To add centring: place the cursor on the first character of the text to be centred and hold down [SHIFT] and press [F6].

Text creation
1 Type [Your Own Name] (to identify printout).
2 Press [RETURN] three times.
3 Type in the text of Task 7.

Amendments
1 Centre the document vertically.
2 Centre each line horizontally.

Check your work and make any necessary corrections. Save the file under [YourInitials7] and print one copy (see page 59).

Task 7

QUALITY TYPING SERVICE

at

reasonable rates

* * * * *

Highly proficient typist
with WORD PROCESSOR
and quality printer
will undertake the typing of

STUDENT DISSERTATIONS, THESES ETC

PERFECTION
G U A R A N T E E D!

For details contact
(Your Own Name)

* * * * *

Task 8

Objective	To underline (underscore) and embolden text when keying in.

Underlining	Press F8 (begin underlining), type the text to be underlined, and then press F8 (end underline).
Emboldening	Press F6 (begin bold), type the text to be emboldened, and then press F6 (end bold).
	Note When using a colour monitor the highlighted text (underlined and/or emboldened) may appear brighter or as a different colour.
Display (reveal) print codes	In order to see where the instructions for underline or bold are, hold down ALT and press F3 (or press F11). The codes are shown in [ ] below the tab ruler line — capital letters for the start and lower case letters for the end.

Memory jogger	Do not press RETURN at the end of a line unless it is the end of a paragraph.
Text creation	1 Type Your Own Name (to identify printout).
	2 Press RETURN three times.
	3 Type in the text of Task 8, underlining the headings, but emboldening the words which are underlined within the passages.
Amendments	No amendments, but check your work thoroughly and correct any typing mistakes you may have made. Save the file under YourInitials8 and print one copy (see page 59).

Task 8

COMMUNICATION

There are many types of communication methods used today, both <u>oral</u> and <u>written</u>.

ORAL COMMUNICATION

This happens all the time when we <u>speak</u> to family, friends or colleagues. Many text books give advice on how to <u>improve</u> communication skills. <u>Oral</u> communication is particularly important when using the <u>telephone</u> so that messages are clearly given and received.

WRITTEN COMMUNICATION

Reports, memos and letters are the most common form of written <u>business</u> communication. <u>Care</u> should be taken to ensure that the <u>meaning</u> of the writer is clear and that the style is <u>appropriate</u> to the circumstances.

Task 9

Objective	To change underlining and emboldening.

Underline text when editing	Place the cursor on the first character to be underlined, hold down ALT and press F4 (or press F12). Press the → arrow key to highlight the text as far as the underline is required to go. Press F8 to cancel the block function and to underline the text just marked.
Embolden text when editing	Place the cursor on the first character to be emboldened, hold down ALT and press F4 (or press F12). Press the → arrow key to highlight the text as far as the bold is required. Press F6 to cancel the block function and to put the marked text in bold.
Remove bold or underline	1 Hold down ALT and press F3 (or press F11) to reveal codes (bottom half of the screen will show the text duplicated with control codes).
	2 Place the cursor on the start code for bold or underline, which is in capital letters, and press DEL.
	3 Repeat step 1 to return to full screen.

Memory jogger	Print codes are shown in [ ] in capital letters for the start and lower case letters for the end.
Text creation	1 Type Your Own Name (to identify printout).
	2 Press RETURN three times.
	3 Type in the text of Task 9, underlining the words as shown.
Amendments	1 Underline all four headings.
	2 First paragraph, first sentence: underline 'pagination'.
	3 First paragraph, second sentence: delete the underlining from 'normally' and 'automatically'.
	4 Second paragraph, first sentence: underline 'page break'.
	5 Third paragraph, first sentence: underline 'override' and delete underlining from 'new'.
	6 Last paragraph, first sentence: delete underlining from 'odd'.
	7 Last paragraph, second sentence: underline 'widow' and 'orphan'.
	8 Last paragraph, last sentence: delete the underlining from 'check' and 'modify'.
	Check your work, save it under filename YourInitials9 and print one copy (see page 59).

Task 9

PAGINATION

One of the terms found in word processing is pagination, which concerns
the number of lines printed per page. Normally you will instruct the
word processor as to the required number of lines in any particular
type of document and your system will automatically insert 'page
breaks' at the specified length.

BREAKS

A page break is in fact a code to the printer to pause during printing.
If you are using continuous stationery the printer will move the paper
up a few lines to leave a gap on either side of the perforation, and
then continue printing the next page.

OVERRIDING

Sometimes you will need to override the automatic page breaks, such as
when there is a relatively small amount of text on your current page
but the next piece is the start of a new section or chapter. This is
known as a hard or forced page break.

WIDOWS/ORPHANS

These somewhat odd terms are straightforward enough. A widow line is
the first line of a paragraph which remains alone at the foot of a
page, and an orphan is the last line of a paragraph which is left all
by itself at the top of a page. It is good practice to check where
your page breaks occur and modify them if necessary.

Task 10

Objective   To create text using indented paragraphs.

Indented paragraphs	Set a tab stop at the required point and press the TAB key (⇥) at the beginning of each paragraph.

Memory jogger

For centred heading before typing, hold down the SHIFT key and press F6. Type the word(s) to be centred. Press RETURN.

To set tab stop: hold down the SHIFT key and press F8. Press 1 (line), press 8 (tab), type the value of the tab to be set and press RETURN (or move the cursor with the arrow key to the required position and press the TAB key). Press F7 twice.

Text creation

1 Type Your Own Name (to identify printout).
2 Press RETURN three times.
3 Set a tab stop at position 1.5″.
4 Type in the text of Task 10, remembering to press the TAB key at the beginning of each paragraph.

Amendments

No amendments, but check your work thoroughly and make any necessary corrections. Print one copy and clear the screen, or save your file under YourInitials10 and print one copy from disk (see page 59).

Task 10

PRINTERS

Word processing systems need to have a printer attached if a paper copy, or hard copy as it is known, is required of any document. Several types are available.

DOT MATRIX

Dot matrix printers produce characters formed of a number of tiny dots and can print at a very high speed.

DAISY WHEEL

Daisy wheel printers are probably the most popular for word processing, as each character around the wheel of the 'daisy' print element strikes the paper and the finished product is similar to work produced on an electronic typewriter.

HIGH SPEED

Very high speeds are achieved with ink jet printing, where ink is sprayed on to the paper in the shape of the characters, and with laser printers, but these are expensive.

DECISION TIME

A business user must decide which printer will best suit the firm's needs, after weighing up the advantages and disadvantages of each.

Task 11

Objective	To use the overtype mode.

> **Overtype mode**   Usually the program is in insert mode, which means that characters are inserted when typed over others. Overtype mode replaces characters without the need to delete them first. Insert ON is the default setting.
>
> 1 Press INS key (bottom right) (this is overtype mode).
> 2 Press INS key to turn insert mode back on.
>
> *Note*   The Status line shows Typeover when Insert is off.

Memory jogger   To underline when editing: place the cursor on the first character to be underlined, hold down ALT and press F4 (or press F11). Press the → arrow key to highlight the text as far as the underline is required. Press F8 to underline the block.

Text creation

1 Type Your Own Name (to identify printout).
2 Press RETURN three times.
3 Type in the text of Task 11.

Amendments

1 First paragraph, first sentence: overtype 'in' with 'by' in 'was in cash'.
2 First paragraph, second sentence: overtype 'still' with 'often', and 'items' with 'goods'.
3 First paragraph, last sentence: overtype 'cash around' with 'actual cash'.
4 Second paragraph, first sentence: overtype 'systems' with 'methods'.
5 Second paragraph, second sentence: overtype 'might' with 'could', and
'dips' with 'goes' in 'dips below a certain amount', and
'shops' with 'firms'.
6 Third paragraph, last sentence: overtype 'off in full' with 'immediately'.
7 Underline the heading.

Check your work to ensure that no typing errors remain. Save the file under YourInitials11 and print one copy (see page 59).

Task 11

METHODS OF PAYMENT

Not long ago the most common form of paying for goods was in cash.
While this is still the case for small items, it is probably more
popular today to pay by cheque or credit card. These are more
convenient and safer than carrying large amounts of cash around.

There are, however, restraints on using these 'cashless' systems. For
example, you might be liable to pay bank charges on each cheque used if
your current account dips below a certain amount and some shops will
not allow you more than £50 worth of goods even with a bank guarantee
card.

There is less of a problem if the shop accepts your credit card, where
you sign in agreement of the sale and are billed later by the credit
card company. This debt can then be paid off in full or on a monthly
basis, but interest will be charged with this monthly method.

Task 12

Objective   To use the line and block delete and restore deleted text.

Delete to end of line (from cursor)   Place the cursor on the first character to be deleted, hold down the CTRL key and press END.

Full line delete   When text has been wrongly keyed, place the cursor on the first character of the line, hold down the CTRL key and press END.

Block delete   Place the cursor on the first character of the text to be deleted, hold down the ALT key and press F4 (or press F12). Use the arrow keys to highlight the text, press DEL and press Y (in answer to question).

Restore deleted text   WordPerfect can hold up to 3 deletions. Place the cursor where the text is to be restored, press F1 and press 1 (to retrieve the most recent text) or 2 (to retrieve previous text).

Memory jogger   If you highlight the wrong piece of text, press F1 to cancel.

Text creation   1 Type Your Own Name (to identify printout).
2 Press RETURN three times.
3 Type in the text of Task 12.

Amendments   1 Using line delete, first paragraph: delete the lines of the last sentence beginning 'This list is known as'.
2 Using block delete, second paragraph: delete the lines of the last sentence beginning 'Under this last item'.
3 Using either method, third paragraph: delete the middle sentence beginning 'However'.
4 Restore your second deletion as the last sentence in the second paragraph.

Check your work for accuracy, save it under filename YourInitials12 and print one copy (see page 59).

Task 12

For a committee meeting to run smoothly it has to be well organised in
advance. This entails informing all the members of the time, date and
venue in good time, usually a minimum of 7 days beforehand, and then
providing a list of the items to be discussed in the order in which
they are to be taken. This list is known as the agenda and is often
sent out with the notice of meeting, along with any relevant documents.

The normal order of the list is first to take any apologies for
absence, then to agree the minutes of the previous meeting and take any
matters arising from them. After that come the items for discussion,
followed by Any Other Business. Under this last item the Chairman has
the right to declare an issue raised by a member to be too important
for unprepared discussion and can request that it be tabled as an
agenda item at the following meeting.

The final point on the agenda is always the date and time of the next
meeting. However, if the committee is disbanding this is not
necessary. Each member of the committee has a copy of the agenda, but
a wise secretary always provides additional copies at the meeting in
case someone has forgotten theirs.

Task 13

Objective	To use the copy and block delete facilities.

<table>
<tr>
<td>Highlight block</td>
<td>Place the cursor on the first character of the text to be marked, hold down <u>ALT</u> and press <u>F4</u> (or press <u>F12</u>). Use the arrow keys to highlight the block (remember to use the arrow key to highlight a line at a time).</td>
</tr>
<tr>
<td>Copy block</td>
<td>Highlight the block as above. Hold down the <u>CTRL</u> key and press <u>F4</u>, press <u>1</u> (for block), press <u>2</u> (to copy). Move the cursor to the new position (it may be on top of text that already exists; do not worry!), press <u>RETURN</u>. The text will appear in both places.</td>
</tr>
<tr>
<td>Block delete
(alternative
method)</td>
<td>Place the cursor on the first character of the text to be deleted, hold down the <u>CTRL</u> key and press <u>F4</u>. To highlight the text press <u>1</u> (for a sentence) or <u>2</u> (for a paragraph) or <u>3</u> (for a page). Press <u>3</u> (to delete).</td>
</tr>
</table>

Memory jogger	See Task 12 for another method of block delete. If you highlight the wrong block, press <u>F1</u> to cancel.
Text creation	1 Type <u>Your Own Name</u> (to identify printout). 2 Press <u>RETURN</u> three times. 3 Type in the text of Task 13.
Amendments	1 Copy the second paragraph and place it after the fifth paragraph. You will now have this paragraph in two places. 2 Delete the original second paragraph. 3 Adjust the line spacing if necessary. 4 Delete the new third paragraph beginning 'In many primary schools'. Check your work, making any necessary corrections. Save the file under filename <u>YourInitials13</u> and print one copy (see page 59).

Task 13

INPUT DEVICES

For word processing operators the usual method of text entry is through a typewriter-style keyboard. There are, however, other ways of entering information into a computer.

In everyday life examples are found in supermarkets, where the bar codes on products are read by laser. This saves the assistant having to key in amounts on a till, and possibly making errors while doing so.

Some games played at home via a television set use a device known as a joystick, and the increasingly popular 'mouse' allows picture representations to be drawn easily on to a screen.

In many primary schools you can see Concept keyboards, which are flat pads over which pictures can be laid so a child has only to press an area of the pad to gain a response from the computer.

There are other devices available involving foot switches or even obeying eye movement which are enormously helpful to handicapped people.

Task 14

Objective	To move paragraphs – block move.

> **Paragraph move (alternative method)** — Place the cursor on the first character of the text to be moved, hold down the CTRL key and press F4. Press 2 (to move a paragraph or 1 for a sentence, 3 for a page). The text is highlighted. Press 1 (to cut/move), move the cursor to the new position, ignoring any text already there, and press RETURN. The paragraph will move.

Memory jogger

To cancel the marked block, press F1.

Text creation

1 Type Your Own Name (to identify printout).
2 Press RETURN three times.
3 Type in the text of Task 14.

Amendments

1 Move the last paragraph so that it becomes the second paragraph.
2 Move what is now your fourth paragraph (beginning 'The Sales or Marketing Department') so that it becomes the last paragraph – make sure there is a blank space between the last line of the text and your cursor when doing the last part of the procedure.

Check your work and make any necessary typing corrections before you save your file under YourInitials14 and print one copy (see page 59).

Task 14

Most organisations divide their responsibilities so that the work is shared according to the functions required to conduct business. For example, a manufacturing firm will probably have three main divisions: Production, Sales and Accounts or Finance.

The Production Department will have to synchronise the arrival of raw materials with the schedule of manufacture planned, which will have been agreed upon with the Sales Department when estimating forecasts of demand.

The Sales or Marketing Department will have responsibility for overseeing staff who may well work out of the office and for determining the price levels to be set.

The job of the Finance Department is to ensure both that debts (to suppliers) and bills (sent to customers) are paid without undue delay and to ensure that the firm remains solvent.

Larger organisations will have many more departments than these three, such as Personnel, Training, Advertising, Management Services, Research and Development, etc.

Task 15

Objective   To split existing paragraphs into more than one.

Paragraph split   1 Position the cursor on the first letter of the sentence which is to become the new paragraph.
2 Press RETURN twice.
3 The paragraph will reformat as you move the cursor down.

Memory jogger   To reveal control codes, press F11 or hold down ALT and press F3.

Text creation   1 Type Your Own Name (to identify printout).
2 Press RETURN three times.
3 Type in the text of Task 15.

Amendments   Change the first paragraph into three shorter ones:

1 New paragraph at 'In a stand alone system'.
2 New paragraph at 'With shared logic'.

In the last paragraph:

3 Make a new paragraph beginning 'However, the'.

Check your work, save it under filename YourInitials15 and print one copy. Delete this file and all previous files (see page 60).

Task 15

Word processing systems are often described as 'stand alone' or 'shared logic'. They can usually perform the same types of tasks but the difference is in the way the equipment is arranged. In a stand alone system, there is a keyboard, a screen, a central processing unit (CPU), disk drive and printer for use by a single operator. In other words, it is a completely self-contained unit. With shared logic, there can be several work stations (ie keyboards with screens) but the logic of the CPU is shared, along with the disk drive and one or more printers.

What this means in practice is that sometimes operators on a shared logic system can experience a short time delay if several people wish to use the same facility at precisely the same time. However, the advantages of shared logic are lower cost for several work stations and greater storage capacity, as their disks usually are of the hard type and can store more information than the floppies used on a stand alone system.

Task 16

Objective	To make single paragraphs from two adjoining ones.

Paragraph join

1 Position the cursor in the space immediately following the full stop in the first paragraph.
2 Press DEL twice (to delete the two RETURNS).
3 Tap the SPACE BAR twice to give 2 spaces after the full stop.
4 The paragraph will reformat as you take the cursor down.

Memory jogger

To add underlining:

1 Position the cursor on first required character.
2 Press F12 (or ALT + F4) and use the cursor keys to highlight the text.
3 Press F8 to add underlining.

To add centring:

1 Position the cursor on the first character of the heading (or text) to be centred.
2 Hold down SHIFT and press F6 .

Text creation

1 Type Your Own Name (to identify printout).
2 Press RETURN three times.
3 Type in the text of Task 16.

Amendments

1 Join the first three paragraphs to become one single paragraph.
2 Join the last two paragraphs to become the second paragraph.
3 Underline and centre the heading.

Check your work for typing corrections, save it under YourInitials16 and print one copy (see page 59).

Task 16

HOUSEKEEPING

The term housekeeping in connection with word processing can be interpreted as filing in the general sense.

Both require that information be stored, be capable of retrieval both by the person who stored it or anyone else permitted to have it, and that old or dead files be disposed of on a regular basis.

With word processing, disposing of unwanted files does not mean throwing away the disks containing them. Instead space is cleared on them for re-use by instructing the computer which files to delete.

Another important difference between housekeeping and filing is that with the former it is advisable to make back-up or security copies of disks in the event that a system failure corrupts the one in use.

It is normally the responsibility of the word processing supervisor to carry out this duty and to decide which disks should be copied.

Task 17

Objective   To input text with a justified right margin and to embolden text.

Justification   A justified right margin has a straight right margin produced when the program inserts extra spaces, making each line the same length.

With the cursor at the top of the document, hold down $\boxed{\text{SHIFT}}$ and press $\boxed{\text{F8}}$. Type $\boxed{1}$ (line), $\boxed{3}$ (justification), $\boxed{\text{Y}}$ (yes) and $\boxed{\text{RETURN}}$ twice.

Note   Justification does not show onscreen, only when the document is printed. It can be viewed before printing: hold down $\boxed{\text{SHIFT}}$ and press $\boxed{\text{F7}}$, then press $\boxed{6}$ (to view). Press $\boxed{\text{F7}}$ to return to document.

Memory jogger   To embolden text when editing, hold $\boxed{\text{ALT}}$ and press $\boxed{\text{F4}}$ (or press $\boxed{\text{F12}}$), move the arrow keys to highlight the appropriate words, and press $\boxed{\text{F6}}$.

Text creation   1 Type $\boxed{\text{Your Own Name}}$ (to identify printout).
2 Press $\boxed{\text{RETURN}}$ three times.
3 Type in the text of Task 17, justifying the right margin.

Amendments   1 First paragraph: embolden 'Health and Safety at Work Act'.
2 Add the title $\boxed{\text{Health and Safety at Work}}$. Make this emboldened and centred.

Check your work, making all necessary corrections, save it under filename $\boxed{\text{YourInitials17}}$ and print one copy (see page 59).

Note   If your work does not print out with a perfectly justified right margin, check that you have not pressed the RETURN key instead of letting the Wordwrap facility make its own line endings. If you have, place your cursor on the space after the last word in the line and press the $\boxed{\text{DEL}}$ key to remove it. The words of the previous line will move to this line. Reform the paragragh.

Task 17

It was with the aim of involving both management and staff in the safeguarding of health and safety standards that the Health and Safety at Work Act was passed in 1974. This meant that for the first time an obligation was placed on employees for the safety interests of themselves and their fellow workers.

Duties of the employer cover the provision of a safe place of work, with safe methods of access and exit, safe equipment and systems of work. There are other requirements of the employer including the protection of visitors to the premises.

Employees must take reasonable care of themselves and of others and refrain from misusing any equipment supplied for safety reasons. The terms of the Act can also make practical jokes a punishable offence if it is believed that harmful results should have been foreseen.

Task 18

Objective	To use the spellcheck facility and count words.

Spellcheck   Save your file before starting spellcheck (press F10). Retrieve a copy of your file.

Start spellcheck   **Hard disk system:** hold CTRL and press F2, press 2 (for page) and follow the screen prompts.

Two floppy disk system: remove the work disk from drive B and insert the speller disk. Hold CTRL and press F2, press 2 (for page) and follow the screen prompts.

Stop spellcheck   Stop spellcheck by pressing F1.

Word count   Hold down CTRL and press F2 (spell). Press 6 (count). Press RETURN twice to return to document.

Memory jogger   Press HOME HOME and ↑ arrow to move to the top of the document.

Text creation   1 Type Your Own Name (to identify printout).
2 Press RETURN three times.
3 Type in the text of Task 18.

Amendments   1 Underline every occurrence of the word 'answerphone'.
2 Entitle the task Answerphones as an underlined, emboldened and centred heading.
3 Starting at the top of the document, switch the spellcheck facility on and check the accuracy of your typing (select 2 for skip if the word 'answerphone' is not recognised).
4 Do a word count of your document and note the number.
5 Add a final sentence: The text on this page contains — words.. (Insert the word count number that you have just found and add 8 for these additional words.)

After checking your work, save it under filename YourInitials18 and print one copy (see page 59).

156

Task 18

Many people are still a little nonplussed if they make a telephone call
and are greeted by a recorded message on an answerphone. If it is
expected that there will be an answerphone service (eg if you ring to
request a catalogue or brochure) then you are prepared and have your
message ready, but it can sometimes be disconcerting to make a call to
a private house and discover that your friends do not answer
themselves.

The procedure is that when an answerphone number rings, the caller is
greeted by a specially recorded message and is invited to speak at the
end of the announcement. This message from the caller is taped and,
whenever convenient, the owner of the answerphone plays back all the
messages. It is not unknown for the caller simply to have gasped at
the end of the recorded announcement, leaving neither message nor name!

Task 19

Objective To use the search and replace feature.

Search and replace	To exchange every occurrence of a word or phrase automatically: 1 Place the cursor at the top of the document, hold down ALT and press F2, press N (to replace automatically) or Y (to replace each occurrence individually). 2 Type the word(s) to be replaced, then press F2. Type the replacement word(s), then press F2. 3 When the search and replace ends, the cursor remains on the last replacement position.

Memory jogger Press HOME HOME and ↑ arrow to move to the top of the document.

Text creation
1 Type Your Own Name (to identify printout).
2 Press RETURN three times.
3 Type in the text of Task 19.

Amendments
1 Replace the name Buckley with Butler.
2 Replace the name Clarke with Clark.

Check the rest of your work and make any necessary typing corrections, print one copy and clear the screen (see page 59).

Task 19

EXTRACT FROM MINUTES OF BOARD MEETING HELD 9 MAY 19--

5   PROFIT AND LOSS STATEMENT

The statement for the previous six months was noted and Mr Buckley
agreed to undertake a revision of budgetary policy.

6   MANAGEMENT SERVICES

Ms Clarke presented her report on the restructuring of the Management
Services Division. Whilst the Board accepted the report in principle,
Ms Clarke and Mr Buckley were directed to discuss the financial
implications further and to present their findings at the next
meeting.

7   COMMUNITY LINKS

The approach by local community workers was outlined by Mr Buckley.
General opinion was in favour of cooperation, but Mr Buckley is to
have further discussions and present a full report at the Annual
General Meeting.

8   DEMAND FORECAST

The forecast was discussed at length, with Ms Clarke believing that
the outlook for autumn could be improved by additional advertising.
It was agreed unanimously to increase the advertising budget by 10%.
Mr Buckley is to put this into effect immediately.

Copy to:
Mr K Buckley
Ms A C Clarke

Task 20

Objective	To use search and replace as an abbreviations facility.

Abbreviations facility	1 During text entry use a symbol (such as @) for the word or phrase you would otherwise have to keep typing, and then replace the symbol with the required word(s) by using Search and replace.
	Note When using this make sure that there are no other occurrences of the symbol you select within the document, otherwise they too will be replaced by the word or phrase you wish to add.
	2 Use Search and replace to insert the required phrase.

Memory jogger

To use Search and replace:

1 Place the cursor at the top of the document, hold ALT and press F2. Press N (to replace automatically) or Y (to replace each occurrence individually).
2 Type the word(s) to be replaced, then press F2. Type the replacement word(s), then press F2.

Text creation

1 Type Your Own Name (to identify printout).
2 Press RETURN three times.
3 Type in the text of Task 20.

Amendments

Replace the '@' symbol with 'Memorandum and Articles of Association'.

Check the rest of your work and make any necessary typing corrections, print one copy and clear the screen (see page 59).

Task 20

The Chairman of the Committee announced that, further to the report of
the working party on the amendments to the @, the finalised draft
could now be produced.

He asked that all members of the Committee read the proposed new @ and
send their written comments to the Secretary by 6 July. The Secretary
would collate all the suggestions in time for the meeting on 13 July,
when a final draft would be prepared.

This draft would then be sent to the solicitors for legal approval
before being sent out to members of the Society during September. The
Chairman hoped this timetable would mean that a proposal to accept the
new @ could be put to the Annual General Meeting of the Society to be
held on 30 January.

The Chairman, appreciating that much time and labour had gone into the
production of the new @, thanked the members of the working party for
their efforts. He hoped the new @ would be considered acceptable by
the Society's members and that the new organisational structure would
result in improved efficiency.

Task 21

Objective   To reformat text that has been keyed in — changing margins — and get a copy of a file already on disk.

Reformatting text	Set new margins above the paragraph where the settings are to take effect. The text will reform to the new settings when it is keyed in or when the cursor is moved down through it (hold down SHIFT and press F8 to format).
Get a copy of file already on disk	1 Hold SHIFT and press F10. 2 Type the drive letter and the filename (eg a:JF16). 3 Press RETURN or 1 Press F5 (to list files), and change the directory if necessary. 2 Use the ↓ arrow to highlight the required file. 3 Press Y (to retrieve). *Note* Always clear the screen before retrieving a copy of a file, unless you want to join files together.

Memory jogger   Justify right margin: hold SHIFT and press F8, press 1 (line), press 3 (justification), type Y, press RETURN three times. *Note* Justification does not show onscreen.

Text creation
1 Type Your Own Name (to identify printout).
2 Press RETURN three times.
3 Type in the text of Task 21. (Or you can amend Task 16 instead, if you have stored it.)

Amendments
1 Inset the second and third paragraphs, using a right-hand margin of 2.5″ and a left-hand margin of 2.5″ set above the second paragraph.
2 Justify these inset paragraphs.
3 Remember to remove the justification and change the ruler settings back for the last paragraph.
4 You will need to check the line setting (hold down SHIFT and press F8, then press 1) at the first line of the second paragraph (with margins of 2.5″ and justify on) and at the first line of paragraph 4 (margins of 1″ and justify off).
5 View before printing: hold down SHIFT and press F7, press 6, press F7 (to return to document).

Check the rest of your work and make any necessary typing corrections, print one copy and clear the screen (see page 59).

Task 21

An Act passed by Parliament in 1978 concerns the various individual rights of people at work and is known as the Employment Protection (Consolidation) Act.

The main points covered in this mean that all employees who work for 16 hours a week or more must be given a written contract of employment within 13 weeks from commencing work. This includes the names of those involved, states the hours of work and what the holiday entitlements are, and other information regarding sickness pay, pension schemes, disciplinary rules, etc.

Employers must also give their staff detailed pay statements showing gross pay, all the deductions and what they were for, and the net pay.

Other items covered in the Act relate to notice to terminate employment, maternity leave, time off work and dismissal procedures.

Task 22

Objective   To inset material within text, using a temporary indent.

Temporary indent

1 Set a tab stop where the indent is required.
2 Press F4 and type the new text or press down arrow ↓ to reform existing text.

Memory jogger   Set tab stop: hold SHIFT and press F8, press 1 (line), press 8 (tab), type the value of the tab to be set and press RETURN. Press F7 twice.

Text creation

1 Type Your Own Name (to identify printout).
2 Press RETURN three times.
3 Type in the text of Task 22, with the material in quotes inset 5 spaces from the left margin.

Amendments   No special amendments, but check your work and correct any typing errors you may have made. Print one copy and clear the screen (see page 59).

Task 22

An interesting exercise is to try to discover how your home town got its name. For example St Helens on Merseyside, noted for its glass making, is an industrial town formerly classed as being in Lancashire. Records show that its name derived from a chapel-of-ease dedicated to St Ellen in about 1540 by the Lord of the Manor of Windle, Windle being one of the four small townships that became the Borough of St Helens.

The growing importance of St Helens in the nineteenth century is shown by the changing descriptions given in commercial directories that provided information concerning the town. One such directory published in 1828 noted that:

'St Helens, although only denominated a village ...'

had within the previous 20 years,

'... so much increased in population and improved in its general appearance that it might be ranked among many of the thriving towns of Lancashire.'

In 1871 St Helens was referred to as:

'a populous and flourishing market town and borough'

and by 1876 as:

'the principal seat of glass manufacture in the United Kingdom.'

Task 23

Objective   To infill variable material in a standard letter and read another file from disk.

Infilling variable material	1 The @ symbol or any other symbol must be inserted at the appropriate points in the standard letter.
	2 Begin the procedure with the cursor at the top of the document by pressing HOME HOME and ↑ arrow.
	3 Use the search option to locate each occurrence of the symbol by pressing F2. Type the symbol to be found (eg @) and press F2 (to begin the search).
	4 The first occurrence of the symbol will be located. Delete it by pressing BACKSPACE DELETE key (← above RETURN key) and type in the appropriate word(s).
	5 Press F2 twice to move to the next occurrence. Repeat step 4.
	6 Continue as above until the last occurrence of the symbol has been changed.

Memory jogger   Get a copy of a file already on disk: hold SHIFT and press F10, type the drive and the filename (eg a:JF23), and press RETURN.

Note   Always clear the screen before retrieving a copy of a file, unless you want to join files together.

Text creation
1 Type Your Own Name (to identify printout).
2 Press RETURN three times.
3 Type in the text of Task 23.

Amendments
1 Save your document with the @ signs under filename YourInitials23.
2 On a clear screen get a copy of your original document.
3 Follow steps 2 to 6 above to insert the following details (one line for each @ symbol):

> Miss G K Anderson
> 49 Southdene Road
> Gidea Park
> ROMFORD
> Essex RM8 2AS
> Miss Anderson
> 12 June

(Continued on page 49.)

Task 23

Ref INT/Your Initials

Today's date

@
@
@
@
@

Dear @

Thank you for your enquiry about our Italian and Spanish courses for the coming session.

There are vacancies on the one-term course you mention and it is possible for fees to be paid on a weekly basis, but this must be arranged before the course commences.

(Continued on page 50.)

Task 23 (continued)

4 Save your file under YourInitials23a and print one copy.

5 Repeat steps 2 to 4 (under Amendments). Insert the details in point 7 below into the standard letter, and name your file YourInitials23b.

6 Repeat steps 2 to 4 (under Amendments). Insert the details in point 8 below into the standard letter, and name your file YourInitials23c.

7
```
Mr G Robinson BA
116 Viking Road
WICKFORD
Essex
SS12 7JA
Mr Robinson
19 June
```

8
```
Ms A C Davies
3 Gleneagles Drive
Oadby
LEICESTER
LE3 5TG
Ms Davies
26 June
```

I feel sure that a visit here would assist you in making a decision, not only so that you may see our facilities but also talk to some of the present course members for their opinions and reactions. If you could visit on Wednesday morning, @, we could have an informal talk over coffee and I would be happy to show you round.

Please let me know by telephone or letter if you would like to come, and the time which would best suit you.

I shall look forward to hearing from you.

Yours sincerely

Your Own Name
Proprietor

Task 24

Objective	To insert blank line spaces during editing.

Inserting blank line spaces retrospectively

If there is already one blank line at the appropriate point (eg between paragraphs):

1 Place the cursor on that blank line.
2 Press RETURN the required number of times.

If blank lines are required within continuous text:

1 Place the cursor on the first character of the text that will follow the blank space.
2 Press RETURN once for each line space required.

Memory jogger

See Task 18 for details of the spellcheck facility.

Text creation

1 Type Your Own Name (to identify printout).
2 Press RETURN three times.
3 Type in the text of Task 24.

Amendments

To allow drawings to be inserted within text:

1 Put 10 blank lines in the second paragraph to follow the wording 'sausage/cigar shape and the small circle)'.
2 After the third paragraph (ending 'wrath of the sun') insert 7 blank lines (the next paragraph begins 'Labels should be').
3 Leave 7 blank lines between the fifth paragraph (ending 'damage to your disk drive') and the last one.

Check the rest of your work and make any necessary typing corrections using the spellcheck, print one copy and clear the screen (see page 59).

Task 24

Care should be exercised when handling floppy disks used on any computer system.

The first important yet obvious point is not to bend, fold or otherwise mutilate a disk or its envelope. The two areas cut into the envelope (the sausage/cigar shape and the small circle) expose the actual disk as does part of the large central hole. These recording surfaces must never be touched.

Disks should be stored in their envelopes in an upright position when not in use and at a temperature between 50 and 100 degrees Fahrenheit to prevent warping. They should not be stored near warm machinery or ventilation inlets and outlets - and of course none should ever be left carelessly on a window sill to face the wrath of the sun.

Labels should be marked prior to being affixed to the envelope and should be of the self sticking, removable type. Only felt-tip pen should be used, not hard pencil or biro pen.

Always make sure that the label on a disk does not project in any way over the edge of the envelope or it could do damage to your disk drive.

Care in disk handling should be part of a fixed routine, along with screen cleaning, etc.

Task 25

Objective	To employ line spacing other than single.

Multiple line spacing

1 Place the cursor at the top of the file or at the point where the new line spacing is required.
2 Hold SHIFT and press F8, press 1 (line), press 6, type the new line spacing number (eg 2 for double), press F7 twice.
3 The appropriate line spacing is displayed onscreen.

Memory jogger

Press F11 (or hold down ALT and press F3) to reveal codes.

Text creation

1 Type Your Own Name (to identify printout).
2 Press RETURN three times.
3 Type in the text of Task 25, using double line spacing.

Amendments

There are no special amendments.

Check your work and correct any typing errors, then print one copy and clear the screen (see page 59).

Task 25

The descriptions hard and soft tend to be used quite a lot in the computer field. Hardware and software are terms which have now passed into everyday language, but if one talks about a 'hard return' in what way does it differ from a 'soft' one?

In fact a soft return is when your word processing system 'makes' a line ending for you. If you then do any editing, such as deleting words, your system will reformat the text and will probably bring text from one line up on to another so as to close any gap.

What is known as a hard return is when you have pressed the RETURN key and thus given a formal instruction for the printer to move up a line space. If you do any deletions on a line which has a hard return at the end, no text will be drawn up from below and any gap will be left. You would need to delete the hard return if you wanted the gap to be closed up.

Task 26

Objective   Wide text and changing pitch.

Wide text

Check whether the wide text facility is available on your printer. If it is:

Hold SHIFT and press F8, press 2 (page), press 8 (paper size). Press 2 or 9 (landscape), press 1 or 8 (paper type). Press RETURN twice.

1 Set appropriate left margin (eg 2").
2 The text will scroll horizontally as you type.

Changing pitch

The default pitch setting is 10 characters to the inch (pica). Change to 12 characters to the inch (elite):

Hold down SHIFT and press F8. Press 3 (document), press 3 (initial font). Use cursor to highlight 12 cpi, press 1 (select), press F7 (to exit to document).

Memory jogger

Embolden text: press F6, type the text, press F6.

Text creation

1 Type Your Own Name (to identify printout).
2 Press RETURN three times.
3 Type in the text of Task 26, using wide text for landscape A4 with margins of 2" and a pitch of 12 characters to the inch.

Amendments

1 Add the heading in bold: INSERT/OVERTYPE MODES.
2 First paragraph, second sentence: after 'any corrections' add '(or alterations)'.
3 Embolden the words 'overtype' and 'insert' each time they occur in the document.

Check your work for accuracy, save it under filename YourInitials26 and print one copy on landscape (longest side to the top) A4 paper (see page 59).

Task 26

Word processing systems operate either in 'overtype' or 'insert' mode
for text entry and editing. The terms are virtually self-explanatory:
in overtype systems any corrections are made by positioning the cursor
at the appropriate point and typing the new characters which will
replace those existing at that point. In insert mode systems, if the
cursor is moved to a point in the text and material typed in, the
characters are inserted as additional material and if these are
intended to be replacements the previous characters must be deleted.

In overtype systems it is possible to enter insert mode, and similarly
with insert systems it is usually easy to enter overtype mode. It is
important, however, to remember to switch off these facilities after
use.

Task 27

Objective   Additional use of tab setting facility.

Memory jogger   Use the tab ruler to change margins and tab settings. Press the TAB key to take you to each of the columns, but press F4 to 'wrap' the final column (see Task 5 for tab settings).

Text creation   1 Type Your Own Name.
                         2 Press RETURN three times.
                         3 Set tabs at 2.7" and 4".
                         4 Type in the text of Task 27.

Amendments   1 Change the heading to unspaced capitals and add 'ABBREVIATED' before it.
                         2 At the appropriate point add 'Monday 26/08/—'. Under the 'Details' column indicate that accommodation is booked for that evening at the Holiday Inn, Vancouver, and that the car must be returned that evening to the Vancouver office.
                         3 Delete the ditto marks and put the required word in full.
                         4 Change the return flight to BA 703A.
                         5 Insert a clear line space between each of the dates.

                         Check your work carefully, save it under filename YourInitials27, print one copy and delete all your files from the disk (see page 60).

Task 27

I T I N E R A R Y

Arrangements for Mr and Mrs D Woodward:

DAY/DATE	TRAVEL	DETAILS
Friday 09/08/--	Flight	1120 Depart Manchester for Toronto (Wardair WD 240) Accom: Royal York Hotel, Toronto
Saturday 10/08/--		Royal York Hotel
Sunday 11/08/--	Coach	1230 Depart Hotel for Niagara, Tour PRS (Return 1900)
Monday 12/08/--	Rail	1015 Depart for Calgary (State Room rail accom)
Wednesday 14/08/--	"	1545 Arrive Calgary Accom: Westward Inn
Thursday 15/08/--	Car Hire	Avis Class II 12 days
Tuesday 27/08/--	Flight	0930 Depart Vancouver for Manchester (Wardair WD 241)

NOTE: all times are local

Saving files; backup files; printing

Filenames A filename consists of the drive letter, a colon, a name of up to 8 characters and an extension of up to 3 characters, eg `a:memo7.JF` (seventh memo produced by JF).

Save file 1 Press `F7`, press `RETURN` (to save), type the drive letter followed by a colon and a name (up to 8 characters), and press `RETURN`, eg `b:JF1` or `a:JF1`.
2 Press `RETURN` (not to exit WP).
3 The file is saved on disk and a clear screen appears ready for the next document.

Save and continue This allows you to save your work and then continue where you left off and is useful when typing a long document:

1 Press `F10`.
2 Type the drive letter, a colon and a filename (eg `b:JF1` or `a:JF1`) and press `RETURN`.
3 If the filename has previously been used, follow the screen prompts and replace the original file with the new version.
4 The document is saved and the text remains onscreen.

Printing Before you print, make sure that the printer is switched on and paper is positioned correctly.

Print from screen Hold down the `SHIFT` key and press `F7`. Press `1` (for full document) or `2` (for a page). The document will print.

Clear screen Press `F7` (to exit). Press `N` (not to save). Press `RETURN` (not to exit WP).

Print from disk If you know the filename: hold down `SHIFT` and press `F7`, press `3` (document on disk), type the drive letter followed by a colon and the filename (eg `a:JF1`), press `RETURN`, then again press `RETURN` (for all pages of document).

If you do not know the name of the file: press `F5` (to list files).

If you need to list the files on the other disk drive, type `=a:` or `=b:` (show list of files) and press `RETURN` twice.

Use the arrow keys to highlight the file chosen, press `RETURN` to print all pages and press `F7` to exit.

Printing while editing

A document other than the one being edited can be printed:

Hold down SHIFT and press F7, type 3 (document on disk), press P, type the drive and filename (eg a:JF1) and press RETURN. Press RETURN (to print all pages) and then press F1 (to return to the screen and continue editing).

Stop printing

1 To cancel printing, hold down SHIFT and press F7, press 4, and press 5 (to stop). Follow the onscreen prompts.
2 To restart, press 4 (to go). Printing will begin at the beginning of the file unless instructed otherwise.

Delete file

1 Press F5 (to list files), type the drive required, ie type =b: (two floppy disk system) or =a: (hard disk system).
2 Press RETURN twice, highlight the name of the required file using the arrow keys, press 2 and press Y (to delete).

Backup file

When a file is called back onscreen, a working copy is placed in the computer memory while the original file remains intact on disk. When the new version of the file has been saved under the original filename, the first version becomes a backup file and has the extension .BK! .

Backup files cannot be directly edited. They must be renamed or copied onto another filename.

Rename file

1 Press F5 (to list files), type the drive required, ie type =b: (two floppy disk system) or =a: (hard disk system).
2 Press RETURN twice, highlight the name of the required file using the arrow keys, press 3 (to rename), type the new filename and press RETURN.

Copy file

1 Press F5 (to list files), type the drive required, ie type =b: (two floppy disk system) or =a: (hard disk system).
2 Press RETURN twice, highlight the name of the required file using the arrow keys, press 8, type a new filename and press RETURN.